●Fun with Engl

Idioms

George Beal
Illustrated by Peter Stevenson

WESTERN ISLES
LIBRARIES
30076045
J423
WITHDRAWN

J423
30076045
SCHOOL
LIBRARY
STOCK

KING*f*ISHER

General editor: John Grisewood
Editor: Nicola Barber
Illustrations: Peter Stevenson
           (Kathy Jakeman Illustration)
Design: Robert Wheeler Associates

KINGFISHER
Kingfisher Publications Plc
New Penderel House, 283–288 High Holborn,
London WC1V 7HZ

This edition published by Kingfisher Publications Plc 2000
10 9 8 7 6 5 4 3 2 1
1(TR)/0100/EDK/(MA)/135EDI

Copyright © Kingfisher Publications Plc 2000

The material in this edition was previously published
by Kingfisher Publications Plc in the *Wordmaster* series
(1993) and in the *Kingfisher Book of Words* (1991)

All rights reserved. No part of this publication may be
reproduced, stored in a retrieval system or transmitted
by any means, electronic, mechanical, photocopying or
otherwise, without the prior permission of the publisher.

A CIP catalogue record for this book is available from
the British Library

ISBN 0 7534 0458 3

Printed in Spain

Idioms are phrases and expressions which are in common use. Most are very familiar, some are amusing, but the majority are not to be taken literally. If you say, 'My heart sank', you do not mean that your heart actually sank, but that you felt depressed because something had gone wrong. 'An itching palm' isn't really itchy. The expression describes someone who is greedy for money. In the following list, each entry is shown with a keyword and the idiom or phrase follows.

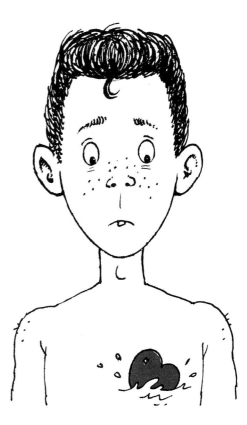

above

above all: especially, most importantly.
above board: openly, honestly, straightforward.
to be above yourself: to be conceited and act in a proud way.

accidents

a chapter of accidents: a series of misfortunes.

accord

of your own accord: without persuasion.

account

to take into account: to allow for, pay attention to.

accounts

by all accounts: according to the information available.

ace

to have an ace up your sleeve: to have a secret idea held in reserve.
within an ace of: close to achieving or doing something.

acid

the acid test: a very severe test to prove something beyond doubt.

across

to get something across: to make something understood.

act

to get caught in the act: to discover someone doing something questionable.
to get in on the act: to join someone in a successful venture.
to put on an act: to behave falsely, to conceal your true feelings.

action

out of action: not working, not in operation.

actions

actions speak louder than words: you are judged more by what you do than by what you say.

Adam
Adam's ale: water.
not know from Adam: to be unacquainted with someone.

advantage
to take advantage of: to use for your own purposes, make good use of.

against
to be up against it: to be in severe trouble.

air
out of thin air: from nowhere, from nothing.

airs
give yourself airs: to be conceited or arrogant.

alive
alive and kicking: alert and active.

all
all in all: when all is considered.
all there: clever, able, bright.

all right
I'm all right, Jack: I'm doing very well (this implies that the speaker is only concerned with him or herself).

alley
a blind alley: a situation or act which leads nowhere.

allowance
make allowance for: to take into consideration.

alone
to go it alone: to do something without any help.

angel
an angel of mercy: someone who helps in a desperate situation.

angels
on the side of the angels: holding the correct moral view.

appearances
to keep up appearances: to continue to behave in a certain way to impress others.

apple
the apple of someone's eye: someone most dear to a person.

apple-cart
to upset the apple-cart: to spoil something which had been planned.

apple-pie
in apple-pie order: everything correct and in place.

Arab
street Arab: a waif or homeless city child.

ark
out of the ark: very old or old-fashioned.

arm
at arm's length: far away, at a certain distance.
to chance your arm: to take a risk.

OUT OF THE ARK

ashes
to rise from the ashes: to build something from destruction.

axe
to have an axe to grind: to have a personal or profitable interest in something.

babe
a babe in arms: someone not very experienced.

baby
to be left holding the baby: to be left to take care of something difficult.

back
to get someone's back up: to annoy someone.
to get your own back: to have your revenge.
to have your back to the wall: to be forced into a defensive position.
to put your back into something: to do something with great enthusiasm and effort.

backwards
to know something backwards: to know something very well.

bad
to go from bad to worse: to become worse than before.
not bad: actually quite good.

bag
a bag of tricks: tools or items needed for a special purpose.
it's in the bag: it's certain or sure.

baker
a baker's dozen: thirteen.

balance
in the balance: touch and go, something not yet decided.

ball
the ball's in your court: it's your responsibility, it's your turn to make a decision.
to keep the ball rolling: to keep a discussion or activity going.
to play ball with: to work with someone, co-operate.

balloon
when the balloon goes up: when something serious occurs.

bananas
to go bananas: to go wild or angry.

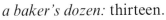

5

bargepole

I wouldn't touch it with a bargepole: I would avoid it in every possible way.

bark

his bark is worse than his bite: someone who appears to be fierce, but who is actually quite gentle.

to bark up the wrong tree: to have a mistaken idea about something.

barrel

to have someone over a barrel: to have someone in a position in which they can do only what you want.

bat

blind as a bat: quite blind.

like a bat out of hell: very fast.

off your own bat: to do something without seeking advice.

be-all

the be-all and end-all: the most important aim or end.

beans

full of beans: lively, vigorous.

to spill the beans: to reveal a secret.

bear

a bear garden: a noisy or unruly place or scene.

bearings

to lose your bearings: to lose your way or direction.

beat

beat about the bush: to delay before saying what you really mean.

beaver

an eager beaver: someone bright, cheerful and enthusiastic.

beck

at someone's beck and call: to be at someone's command.

animal idioms

Many idioms use mammals or birds in a colourful way. Here are a few:

bats in the belfry: slightly mad.
the bee's knees: someone who thinks they are superior.
raining cats and dogs: raining hard.
in the dog-house: in disgrace.
dog-in-the-manger: someone with a grudging and unwilling attitude.
a dog's dinner: a mess.
donkey's years: a long time.
to get someone's goat: to annoy someone.
to be up with the lark: to get up early.

bed

to get out of bed on the wrong side: to begin a day badly.

bee

to have a bee in your bonnet: to persist in pursuing a single idea.

beeline

to make a beeline: to make directly for someone or something.

beggars

beggars can't be choosers: people in need can only accept what is offered.

bell

as clear as a bell: easily heard.

as sound as a bell: in good condition or working order.

to ring a bell: to recall a distant memory.

belt

below the belt: unfair, not following the rules.

to tighten your belt: to spend less in order to save money.

benefit

benefit of the doubt: to treat someone as innocent, despite your doubts.

best

the best of both worlds: taking advantage of two different situations.

better

to get the better of someone: to overcome or win.
to have seen better days: to be in a worse condition than before.

bird

the bird has flown: someone has escaped.

bite

to bite off more than you can chew: to take on more than you can really cope with.
to bite someone's head off: to shout angrily at someone.

bitter

a bitter pill to swallow: an unpleasant fact that has to be accepted.

blessing

a blessing in disguise: good fortune coming from an apparent evil.

block

a chip off the old block: a child who takes after one of his or her parents.

blood

to act in cold blood: to do something callously.
blood is thicker than water: family ties are strong and should be preferred to outside loyalties.
to make someone's blood boil: to make someone very angry.
to make someone's blood run cold: to horrify someone.

blue

blue-eyed boy: a favourite.
a bolt from the blue: something unexpected.
once in a blue moon: very rarely.

board

to sweep the board: to carry off all the prizes.

boat

in the same boat: in the same situation.
don't rock the boat: don't spoil things which are pleasant or comfortable.

boats

to burn your boats: to allow yourself no means of retreat.

bolt

to make a bolt for it: to run away or escape.

bone

dry as a bone: very dry.
to have a bone to pick with someone: to have something to complain or quarrel about.

bones

to make no bones about: to say openly and without hesitation.

book

by the book: according to the rules.
to read someone like a book: to understand someone's character.

books

to be in someone's good books: to be in favour with someone.

boots

too big for your boots: to think too highly of yourself.

bow

to have two strings to your bow: not to depend on one person or thing.

brains

to pick someone's brains: to find out what someone thinks about something.
to rack your brains: to think hard about something.

brass

to get down to brass tacks: to deal with the main points.

bread

to know which side your bread is buttered on: to know where your best interests lie.

breast

to make a clean breast of it: to confess everything.

breath

to take your breath away: to astound.
with bated breath: very excited and anxious.
under your breath: in a whisper.

bricks

like a ton of bricks: very harshly and heavily.

broad

as broad as it's long: whichever way it's considered, it makes no difference.

broom

a new broom: someone in a new situation who starts off with great energy and enthusiasm.

brow

by the sweat of your brow: by hard work.

brush

tarred with the same brush: having the same faults and qualities.

buck

to pass the buck: to pass responsibility onto someone else.

bud

to nip in the bud: to put a stop to something before it has really begun.

bull

like a bull in a china shop: behaving in a rough, coarse, clumsy way.

bundle

to be a bundle of nerves: to be in a very nervous, agitated state.

burn

to burn the candle at both ends: to work and play hard.
to burn the midnight oil: to study or work until late into the night.

bushel

to hide your light under a bushel: to be modest and unassuming.

busman

a busman's holiday: leisure time spent doing the same thing as you do at work.

butter
butter wouldn't melt in his mouth:
applied to someone who looks innocent
but probably isn't.

cake
a piece of cake: something easy to do.
to have your cake and eat it: to have it
both ways.

cakes
to sell like hot cakes: to sell very
quickly.

calf
to kill the fatted calf: to give a special
welcome to someone.

cards
to-play your cards close to your chest: to
be secretive.
to put your cards on the table: to be
honest and reveal all.

cart
to put the cart before the horse: to do
things in the wrong order.

castles
to build castles in the air: to think up
imaginary ideas or schemes.

cat
not room to swing a cat: describes a
cramped area.
to let the cat out of the bag: to reveal
secret or important news.
to put the cat amongst the pigeons: to
cause trouble and confusion.

chalk
as different as chalk from cheese: very
different indeed.
not by a long chalk: far from it; not by
any means.

cheek
to speak tongue in cheek: to speak
mockingly or insincerely.

cheese
hard cheese!: bad luck!

cherry
to have two bites at the cherry: to have
two attempts at the same thing.

chest
to get something off your chest: to talk
about your problems.

chicken
chicken-feed: something of little value.

choice
Hobson's choice: no choice at all.

cloak
cloak and dagger: secret, undercover.

close
a close shave: a narrow escape.

coast
the coast is clear: there's no danger
now.

CROCODILE TEARS

coil
to shuffle off this mortal coil: to die.

colour
off colour: to feel slightly ill.
that's a horse of a different colour: that's quite a different matter.

colours
under false colours: under a false identity.
nail your colours to the mast: to refuse to surrender.

comfort
cold comfort: no comfort at all.

cook
to cook the books: to falsify accounts.

cookie
that's the way the cookie crumbles: you must accept things as they are.

Coventry
send to Coventry: to ignore someone.

creeps
he gives me the creeps: describes a feeling of dislike for, and fear of, someone.

crocodile
crocodile tears: fake tears or sorrow.

cropper
to come a cropper: to fall, usually heavily.

crow
as the crow flies: in a straight line, direct.

crumbs
crumbs from the rich man's table: small trifles given by the rich to the poor.

cud
to chew the cud: to contemplate or think deeply.

cupboard
cupboard love: false affection for material gain.

cut
cut and dried: inflexible and predictable.
to cut a long story short: to leave out the details and get straight to the point.
to cut off your nose to spite your face: to do something in anger which is actually going to cause you more harm.

daggers
at daggers drawn: hostile, quarrelling or fighting.

dance
to lead someone a dance: to cause someone trouble before making a final decision.

dark
to keep dark about something: to keep something a secret.

day
to call it a day: to decide to end something.

deaf

deaf as a post: very deaf.
to fall on deaf ears: to be unheeded.

deep

to go off the deep end: to get angry and express yourself strongly.

devil

between the devil and the deep sea: stuck between two unpleasant options.

diamond

a rough diamond: a rough person with good qualities.

dice

to dice with death: to perform some dangerous feat.

do

to do someone down: to cheat someone.
to do something up: to restore or repair something.

dog

a dog's dinner: a mess.
dog-tired: very tired.
to lead a dog's life: to have a miserable time.

dogs

go to the dogs: to go to ruin and neglect.
let sleeping dogs lie: to leave well alone.

donkey

donkey's years: a very long time.
he can talk the hind leg off a donkey: someone who talks too much and for too long.

down

down and out: penniless and homeless.

dudgeon

in high dudgeon: angered or annoyed.

dust

to throw dust in someone's eyes: to try to deceive someone.

ear

to get a flea in your ear: to be told off or scolded.

ears

wet behind the ears: lacking in experience.

earth

down-to-earth: practical, plain-spoken.
to the ends of the Earth: anywhere.

easier

easier said than done: it's easier to say how something should be done than actually do it.

eat

to eat like a horse: to eat a lot.

11

WHAT'S EATING YOU?

eating
what's eating you?: what's the matter?

egg
a bad egg: a rascal, someone worthless or unreliable.
to have egg on one's face: to appear foolish.

eggs
to put all your eggs in one basket: to risk everything on one venture.

elbow
elbow grease: hard work.
to give someone the elbow: to get rid of someone.

end
to come to a sticky end: to finish unpleasantly.

to keep your end up: to survive under difficulty.

errand
a fool's errand: a purposeless journey.

even
to get even with someone: to have your revenge.

event
to be wise after the event: to offer advice about something after it's happened.

exhibition
to make an exhibition of yourself: to behave foolishly before others.

eye
easy on the eye: attractive to look at.
turn a blind eye to: to ignore an action or behaviour.

eyelid
not to bat an eyelid: to show no surprise or emotion.

eyes
a sight for sore eyes: something very pleasant to look at.
to keep your eyes skinned: to keep a close watch.
up to your eyes: completely.

face
put a good face on it: to appear to be happy while unhappy.
to face up to something: to accept a situation bravely.
to keep a straight face: to keep serious in an amusing situation.
to face the music: to confront the consequences of an action.

fair

fair and square: honest and correct.

fall

to fall for: 1. to be deceived, 2. to fall in love with.

false

to sail under false colours: to pretend to be something you aren't in order to gain benefit.

fancy

to take someone's fancy: to take a liking to something or someone.

far

to go too far: to do something unacceptable.

fast

fast and furious: suddenly and quickly.

fat

the fat is in the fire: what has happened can't be changed and the consequences must be accepted.

feather

a feather in your cap: something of which you can be proud.
birds of a feather: people with common interests and tastes.
to feather your nest: to become rich slyly and secretly.
to show the white feather: to be a coward.

feet

to have cold feet: to worry whether you are making the right decision.
to land on your feet: to have good luck.
to stand on your own feet: to be independent.
to sweep someone off their feet: to make a great impression on someone.

fence

to sit on the fence: to remain neutral.

few

few and far between: uncommon, rare.

fiddle

fit as a fiddle: very healthy.
play second fiddle to: to occupy an inferior position to someone.

field

to have a field-day: to enjoy yourself a great deal.

fight

fight tooth and nail: to fight ferociously or with determination.

finger

to have a finger in the pie: to be involved in something.
to twist someone around your little finger: to be able to control or influence someone.

fingers

to be all fingers and thumbs: to be clumsy and awkward.
to burn your fingers: to come off badly.

fingertips

at your fingertips: to be very familiar with something.

fire

to play with fire: to take unnecessary risks.

fish

like a fish out of water: to feel awkward in a strange situation or place.
to have other fish to fry: to have something better to do.

flash

a flash in the pan: something which lasts only a short while.

flat

in a flat spin: in a state of mental confusion.

13

fly

fly in the ointment: a small problem or difficulty.

food

food for thought: something worthy of consideration.

fool

to make a fool of someone: to make someone appear silly or stupid.

foot

to have a foot in both camps: to have an interest in both sides.
to put your foot down: to assert your authority.
to put your foot in it: to make an embarrassing mistake.

footloose

footloose and fancy free: free to do anything or go anywhere.

footsteps

to follow in someone's footsteps: to do something which has been done before.

form

true to form: acting in a characteristic manner.

fort

to hold the fort: to look after something while the person in charge is away.

foul

to fall foul of: to have a disagreement with.

frog

to have a frog in your throat: to speak huskily.

frying-pan

to jump from the frying-pan into the fire: to escape from one danger only to encounter a worse one.

furrow

to plough a lonely furrow: to work alone.

gab

the gift of the gab: being able to talk easily and confidently.

gaff

to blow the gaff: to betray a secret to someone in authority.

game

to give the game away: to let a secret out.
to play the game: to behave fairly and honourably.

gate-post

between you and me and the gate-post: in strict confidence.

ghost
the ghost of a chance: a very slim chance.

gingerbread
to take the gilt off the gingerbread: to reduce the value of something.

give
to give as good as you get: to retaliate as strongly as you are attacked.

gloves
to handle with kid gloves: to treat gently.

glutton
a glutton for punishment: someone who seems to like doing difficult or dangerous tasks.

go
to make a go of something: to make a success of something.

going
to find something heavy going: to find difficulty in making progress.

A FROG IN THE THROAT

gold
to have a heart of gold: to be very kind-hearted.

good
good for nothing: someone useless or worthless.
good Samaritan: someone who gives help to another.
to be up to no good: to be doing something mischievous or wrong.

goose
to cook someone's goose: to ruin someone's chances.

gooseberry
to play gooseberry: to be an unwelcome third when two people want to be alone.

gospel
to take as gospel: to accept something completely.

grace
to fall from grace: to lose favour.
with bad grace: unwillingly.

grade
to make the grade: to succeed.

grain
against the grain: against a natural tendency.

granted
to take something for granted: to assume that something will take place without evidence that it will.

grass
don't let the grass grow under your feet: don't lose time in setting to work.

grave
one foot in the grave: to be old and feeble, near death.
to dig your own grave: to make a situation bad for yourself.

15

Greek
it's all Greek to me: it's too difficult for me to understand.

grief
to come to grief: to meet with disaster.

grin
to grin and bear it: to put up with misfortune without complaint.

grindstone
to keep your nose to the grindstone: to keep working without rest.

guess
your guess is as good as mine: I know no more about it than you.

gum
to be up a gum tree: to be in a really bad situation.

gun
to jump the gun: to be too hasty.

hair
a hair's breadth: a tiny distance.
to get in someone's hair: to annoy someone.
to let your hair down: to relax and enjoy yourself.

hairs
to split hairs: to get involved in unimportant details.

hand
an old hand: someone with experience.
don't bite the hand that feeds you: don't be ungrateful to someone who has helped you.
hand in glove: to be on intimate terms with someone.
hand over fist: in large amounts.
to get your hand in: to practise.

handle
to fly off the handle: to lose your temper.

hands
to be in good hands: to be well looked after.
to take your life in your hands: to risk death.
to wash your hands of something: to disclaim responsibility.

hang
to get the hang of something: to understand the principle of something.

hard
hard done by: badly treated.

BITING THE HAND THAT FEEDS YOU

LION FOOD

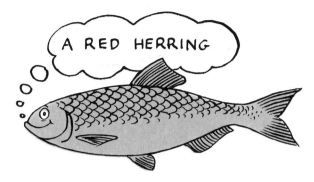

A RED HERRING

harm
out of harm's way: no longer in a position to cause danger.

hash
to make a hash of something: to ruin a job or project.

hat
at the drop of a hat: right away.
I'll eat my hat: an expression of astonishment.
old hat: out of date.
to keep something under your hat: to keep something secret.
to take your hat off to someone: to show admiration.
to talk through your hat: to talk without real knowledge of something.

hatchet
to bury the hatchet: to end a quarrel.

have
to have it in for someone: to set out to cause harm to someone.
to have it out with someone: to discuss and settle a dispute.

hay
to hit the hay: to go to bed or to sleep.

head
to have a good head on your shoulders: to have good judgment and discretion.
to have a level head: to be sensible and calm.

to keep your head above water: to keep out of debt.
to lose your head: to act stupidly in a crisis.
unable to make head or tail of: unable to understand.

headway
to make headway: to make progress.

heart
my heart bleeds for you: I am very sorry for you.
to break your heart: to feel deep disappointment.
to have your heart in the right place: to be kind and sympathetic.
to take heart: to feel encouraged.
to take something to heart: to feel deeply pained about something.
to wear your heart on your sleeve: to show your feelings openly.

heat
in the heat of the moment: action without thought.

heaven
in seventh heaven: in a state of happiness and perfect bliss.
move heaven and earth: to make every effort.
smell to high heaven: to smell very bad.

heels
to show a clean pair of heels: to escape.

hell
come hell or high water: whatever may happen.
hell for leather: very fast.

herring
a red herring: a false clue or trail.

hiding
he was on a hiding to nothing: he had no chance at all of succeeding.

17

hills
as old as the hills: very old.

hog
to go the whole hog: to do something completely and wholeheartedly.

hold
to hold good: to be valid.
to hold in check: to restrain or control.
to hold water: to stand up to close inspection.

holes
to pick holes in something: to find fault with something.

home
to bring something home to someone: to make something fully understood.

hop
to catch someone on the hop: to do something to someone when they are least prepared.

horse
a dark horse: someone who does something unexpected.
to flog a dead horse: to go on discussing something when everyone else has lost interest.
to back the wrong horse: to support the wrong person or party.
to get on your high horse: to be self-righteous and arrogant.

hot
to blow hot and cold: to be enthusiastic and critical by turns.

hour
at the eleventh hour: just in time.

houses
as safe as houses: completely safe.

humble
to eat humble pie: to apologize abjectly.

ice
to break the ice: to ease a first meeting between people.
to cut no ice: to make no impression upon someone.
to put on ice: to postpone.

insult
to add insult to injury: to cause additional trouble to someone.

iron
to rule with a rod of iron: to control someone very strictly.

ivory
an ivory tower: studies or interests which isolate you from other people.

Jack
Jack of all trades: someone who does many jobs but few well.

jam

in a jam: in a difficult situation.

joke

beyond a joke: no longer funny.

justice

to do justice to: to treat something as it deserves.

keel

on an even keel: calm, steady and untroubled.

ken

beyond our ken: outside our understanding or knowledge.

kettle

a pretty kettle of fish: a muddle or confused state of affairs.
the pot is calling the kettle black: you're criticizing others for faults you have yourself.

kill

dressed to kill: smartly dressed.
to kill two birds with one stone: to gain two objectives with one effort.

killing

to make a killing: to make a large profit.

kingdom

until kingdom come: for a long time.

knock

knock the bottom out of: to prove that a theory or statement is quite false.

knuckle

to knuckle under: to give in, yield.

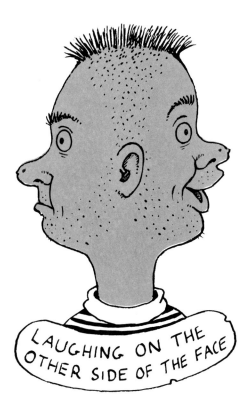

LAUGHING ON THE OTHER SIDE OF THE FACE

knuckles

to rap someone over the knuckles: to reprimand.

lamb

like a lamb to the slaughter: quietly, without being aware of any danger.

lap

in the lap of the gods: left to chance.

laugh

to have the last laugh: to have your opinions justified in the end.
to laugh on the other side of your face: to be humiliated.

19

law

to be a law unto yourself: to disregard the advice and rules of others.

lead

to lead someone on: to encourage someone by offering false hopes.

leaf

to take a leaf from someone's book: to follow someone's example.
to turn over a new leaf: to reform and start afresh.

leaps

by leaps and bounds: to grow or progress very quickly.

leg

not have a leg to stand on: to have no defence.
to pull someone's leg: to make fun of someone, by telling them something untrue.

light

a leading light: someone important and well-known.
to come to light: to appear or be revealed.
to go out like a light: to drop off to sleep quickly.

lily

to gild the lily: to try to improve something which is already attractive.

linen

to wash your dirty linen in public: to discuss your private business publicly.

lines

to read between the lines: to understand something which is implied.

lion

the lion's share: the largest part.

log

as easy as falling off a log: very easy.

look

to look up to someone: to respect someone highly.

loose

at a loose end: having nothing to do.

love

there is no love lost between them: they dislike each other.

low

to lie low: to hide.

luck

as luck would have it: by fortunate chance.
to push your luck: to take risks.

lurch

to leave in the lurch: to abandon.

luxury

to live in the lap of luxury: to live in comfort and wealth.

mad

mad as a hatter: quite crazy.

make

to make do with something: to use something inferior instead of something better.
to make ends meet: to live within your income.

mark

to be quick off the mark: to be alert and quick to respond.
to be up to the mark: to be of the standard required.

matter

a matter of life and death: something of great importance and urgency.

TO BREATHE DOWN SOMEONE'S NECK

meal

to make a meal of something: to make a fuss over something.

mealy

mealy-mouthed: afraid to speak out.

mill

to go through the mill: to endure hard and vigorous training.

million

one in a million: someone or something which is the best of its kind.

mince

don't mince matters: speak plainly and frankly.

mind

to have a good mind to do something: to intend to do something.
to have a mind of your own: to be able to think for yourself.

money

money for old rope: money easily obtained.

monster

the green-eyed monster: jealousy.

mountain

to make a mountain out of a molehill: to exaggerate a problem.

mouth

down in the mouth: distressed or unhappy.

nail

to hit the nail on the head: to understand exactly.

neck

to breathe down someone's neck: to be close behind someone.
neck and neck: equal.

needle

finding a needle in a haystack: attempting to do the impossible.

21

nerve

to lose your nerve: to become afraid.

nerves

to get on someone's nerves: to irritate someone.

nest

a nest egg: savings put aside.

nettle

to grasp the nettle: to attack a difficulty with boldness.

nick

in the nick of time: at the last possible moment.

nines

dressed up to the nines: dressed in your best clothes.

nineteen

to talk nineteen to the dozen: to chatter continuously.

nodding

to have a nodding acquaintance: to know someone or something slightly.

nose

to keep your nose clean: to keep out of trouble.
to put someone's nose out of joint: to offend someone.
to pay through the nose: to pay a high price for something.
to turn your nose up at something: to treat with contempt.

numbered

someone's days are numbered: someone or something will not last for long.

nut

a hard nut to crack: a very difficult problem.

nutshell

in a nutshell: very briefly.

oar

to stick your oar in: to interfere.

off

on the off chance: with a slight possibility that something might happen.

over

over my dead body: not if I can prevent it happening!
over and done with: quite finished.

overboard

to go overboard for something: to be enthusiastic about something.

own

to hold your own: to survive against opposition.

oyster

the world is your oyster: to be able to get what you enjoy from life.

p's and q's

to mind your p's and q's: to be polite and well-behaved.

paces

to put someone through their paces: to test someone's ability.

pains

to take pains: to go to a lot of trouble.

paint

to paint the town red: to enjoy life heartily and noisily.

pale

beyond the pale: outside the limits of decent society.

palm

to have an itching palm: to have a great desire for money.

pants

to bore the pants off someone: to be utterly boring.

pass

to come to a pretty pass: to be in a bad state.
to come to pass: to happen.

path

lead up the garden path: to entice or mislead.

pay

to pay your way: to live free of debt.

peacock

proud as a peacock: vain.

pearls

to cast pearls before swine: to offer something of worth to someone unappreciative.

pebble

you're not the only pebble on the beach: there are plenty of others besides you.

pedestal

to put someone on a pedestal: to have such a great admiration for someone.

peg

a square peg in a round hole: someone in an unsuitable job.
to take someone down a peg: to humiliate someone.

penny

in for a penny, in for a pound: once you've started on something it's best to continue to the end.

to turn up like a bad penny: said of someone unwanted who frequently reappears.

petard

hoist with his own petard: someone caught in a trap which they set to catch others.

PEARLS BEFORE SWINE

Peter

to rob Peter to pay Paul: to pay one person at another's expense.

pillar

from pillar to post: from one refuge to another.

pinch

to feel the pinch: to undergo hardship through lack of money.

plunge

to take the plunge: to take a decision on something risky.

23

colour idioms

Many idioms use colours in a descriptive way. Here are some examples:

in the black: in credit.
the future looks black: the future doesn't look promising.
black looks: disapproving glances.
to scream blue murder: to scream loudly.
out of the blue: completely unexpected.
to feel blue: to be depressed.
once in a blue moon: very rarely.
to have green fingers: someone who is good at growing plants.
a red-carpet reception: a lavish welcome.
to paint the town red: to enjoy a night out.
to catch someone red-handed: to catch someone as they are doing something wrong.

pocket
out of pocket: put to expense.

point
not to put too fine a point on it: to speak bluntly.

posted
to keep someone posted: to supply information to someone regularly.

practise
to practise what you preach: you should behave as you tell others to behave.

praise
to damn with faint praise: to praise something so slightly that it amounts to criticism.

presence
presence of mind: having your wits about you.

pressure
to bring pressure to bear: to force someone to do something.

pride
to put your pride in your pocket: to be humble.

pudding
the proof of the pudding is in the eating: only using something decides how useful it is.

pull
to pull through: to succeed with difficulty.

Punch
as pleased as Punch: very pleased.

purposes
at cross purposes: to misunderstand one another's intentions.

put
hard put to it: in great trouble.
to put in a word: to use your influence.
to put off: to postpone.
to put two and two together: to realize something.
to put up with: to suffer.

question
out of the question: not to be considered.

quick
cut to the quick: deeply hurt.

rain
as right as rain: perfectly well.

rainbow

to chase a rainbow: to think and go after impossible things.

rainy

to keep something for a rainy day: to put something aside in case you may need it later.

rat

to smell a rat: to suspect that something is wrong.

record

to set the record straight: to make sure that any mistake has been rectified.

red

to be in the red: to be in debt.
to see red: to become angry.

rhyme

without rhyme or reason: inexplicably.

ring

to ring the changes: to introduce a new idea.

rise

to take a rise out of someone: to amuse yourself by making someone angry or excited.

rock

steady as a rock: dependable.

Rome

Rome wasn't built in a day: important things cannot be done in a short time.
when in Rome, do as the Romans do: behave like the locals.

roof

to go through the roof: to be very angry.

roost

to come home to roost: refers to a misdeed or mistake which eventually affects the sinner.

A SMELLY RAT

ropes

to know the ropes: to know how to do a particular job.

roses

no bed of roses: a far from comfortable place or situation.

rough

to take the rough with the smooth: to accept set-backs as calmly as you accept good fortune.

roughshod

to ride roughshod: to treat someone harshly and insensitively.

rub

to rub someone up the wrong way: to irritate or upset someone.

rug

to pull the rug from under someone: to cease giving support or help to someone.

25

sack

to get the sack: to be dismissed from employment.
to hit the sack: to go to bed or to sleep.

sailing

plain sailing: to continue without difficulty.

salt

salt of the earth: a thoroughly dependable person.

scarce

to make yourself scarce: to vanish or go away.

scenes

behind the scenes: in private.

school

to tell tales out of school: to reveal private or secret information.

scot

scot-free: quite uninjured.

scratch

to start from scratch: to start from the beginning.

secret

an open secret: a secret which everyone knows.

serve

to serve someone right: to be the right punishment for someone.

set

to set about: to commence.

shadow

not a shadow of doubt: no doubt at all.

sheet

to start with a clean sheet: to start anew.

shell

to come out of your shell: to become more bold and confident.

ship

when your ship comes in: when your fortune is made.

ships

ships that pass in the night: people that meet once and never meet again.

shoes

to step into someone's shoes: to take someone's place.

shop

to talk shop: to talk about business affairs.

shoulder

to give someone the cold shoulder: to be deliberately unfriendly to someone.

shoulders

to be head and shoulders above: far above, or superior to others.

silver

to be born with a silver spoon in your mouth: to be born well-off.

six

six of one and half a dozen of the other: there is no difference or real choice.

sixes

all at sixes and sevens: in a state of disorder or confusion.

skates

to get your skates on: to hurry.

skeleton

skeleton in the cupboard: a secret, usually something of which a person or family is ashamed.

sleep

to sleep like a log: to sleep very soundly.

YOU'RE A SPADE!

sleeve

to have something up your sleeve: to have a secret plan which can be used in an emergency.

slip

to give someone the slip: to escape secretly.

smoke

put that in your pipe and smoke it: listen to that and think over it.

there's no smoke without fire: if something is discussed or mentioned, there's usually a good reason for it.

snake

a snake in the grass: a traitor and deceiver.

song

to buy something for a song: to buy something cheaply.

to make a song and dance about something: to make a great fuss.

sorts

out of sorts: not well.

spade

to call a spade a spade: to speak plainly and frankly.

spanner

to throw a spanner in the works: to ruin a plan.

spoil

to spoil for a fight: to be keen to fight.

spoke

to put a spoke in someone's wheel: to hinder someone.

spring

full of the joys of spring: cheerful and happy.

square

back to square one: back to the beginning.

27

stand

to stand up for: to support.

steal

to steal a march upon: to gain an advantage over someone.

steam

to let off steam: to give full expression to your feelings.

steamed

to get steamed up: to be angry or upset.

stick

in a cleft stick: in a dilemma.
to stick up for: to support or defend someone.

stomach

to turn your stomach: something that makes you feel sick.

stone

leave no stone unturned: make every effort to do something.
to have a heart of stone: to be hard-hearted.

stools

fall between two stools: to be neither one thing nor another.

storm

a storm in a teacup: big excitement over something very unimportant.

street

right up someone's street: to be exactly right for someone.

strides

to make great strides: to make good progress.

strike

strike while the iron is hot: don't miss a welcome opportunity.

study

in a brown study: completely absorbed in thought.

sweep

to sweep something under the carpet: to hide or keep secret something unpleasant.

swoop

at one fell swoop: in a single movement.

tables

to turn the tables on: to reverse the position of two rivals.

tastes

there's no accounting for tastes: everyone has their own likes and dislikes.

teeth

to escape by the skin of your teeth: to have a very narrow escape.
to get your teeth into something: to tackle something seriously.
to set your teeth on edge: something which irritates you.

tenterhooks

to be on tenterhooks: to feel impatient and anxious.

terms

to come to terms with something: to accept a state of affairs.

tether

at the end of your tether: to reach the end of your resources.

thick

thick as thieves: very friendly.

TOFFEE-NOSED

thunder

to steal someone's thunder: to spoil the effect of someone's performance by doing beforehand what they intended.

time

for the time being: for the present.
in less than no time: very soon.

toast

warm as toast: comfortably warm.

toffee

toffee-nosed: snobbish or snooty.

tongue

on the tip of your tongue: to be just about to say something.
to hold your tongue: to stay silent.
a slip of the tongue: something said by mistake.

tooth

to have a sweet tooth: to like eating sweet things.

Tom

Every Tom, Dick and Harry: anyone at all.

thorn

to be a thorn in someone's flesh: to cause someone a lot of trouble.

thread

to hang by a thread: to be in a dangerous situation.

threads

pick up the threads: to go back to something after a period of lapse.

thumb

to stick out like a sore thumb: to be obviously out of place.
to be under the thumb of someone: to be totally controlled by someone.

thumbs

thumbs up; thumbs down: acceptance; rejection.

A SWEET TOOTH

top

to blow your top: to be very angry.

torch

to carry a torch for someone: to be in love with someone.

towel

to throw in the towel: to admit defeat.

tower

a tower of strength: a reliable and trustworthy person.

trumpet

blow your own trumpet: to sing your own praises.

tune

to the tune of: to the amount of.

twinkling

in the twinkling of an eye: in an instant.

unstuck

to come unstuck: to fail.

untimely

to meet with an untimely end: to die prematurely.

up

to be up to something: to be occupied in some pursuit.

uptake

quick (or slow) on the uptake: quick (or slow) to understand.

vengeance

with a vengeance: extremely.

WARTS AND ALL

voice

at the top of your voice: very loudly.

wall

go to the wall: to fail.

wanting

to be found wanting: lacking an important quality.

warts

warts and all: with all the bad points as well as the good ones.

wash

to come out in the wash: to come to a satisfactory end.

water

in hot water: in trouble.
to pour cold water on: to dampen enthusiasm.

waters

pour oil on troubled waters: to bring a quarrel to an end by gentle persuasion.

way

to get your own way: to have or do what you want.

make way: to stand aside.

wayside

to fall by the wayside: to fail in your endeavour.

weather

under the weather: unwell and not very cheerful.

wedge

the thin end of the wedge: the creation of a dangerous precedent.

weight

to pull your weight: to do a fair share of the work.

to throw your weight about: to be domineering.

whip

to have the whip hand: to have control over something or someone.

whisper

a stage whisper: a whisper that can be heard by everyone.

whistle

to wet your whistle: to have a drink.

white

a white lie: a lie which does no harm, or which is used in politeness.

a white elephant: something which has outlived its usefulness.

whole

the whole shooting match: everything, the whole lot.

wind

to have the wind up: to be afraid.

to sail close to the wind: to come close to causing offence.

wing

to take someone under your wing: to protect.

winks

to have forty winks: to have a nap or short sleep.

wits

at your wits' end: confused and perplexed; not knowing what to do.

wolf

to cry wolf: to give a false warning of danger.

to keep the wolf from the door: to keep yourself alive.

wonder

a nine days' wonder: something which attracts interest but which is soon forgotten.

wonders

wonders will never cease: an expression of surprise at something happening.

wood

not to see the wood for the trees: so concerned with detail that you fail to notice the main idea.

wool

to pull the wool over someone's eyes: to deceive someone.

word

to keep your word: to keep your promise.

to take someone's word for it: to believe what someone says without checking.

words

words fail me: to be too shocked to say anything.

world

on top of the world: very happy and cheerful.

out of this world: excellent.

worth

to be worth your salt: to be deserving of reward through diligence and hard work.

writing

writing on the wall: an event which foretells future difficulties or problems.

year

since the year dot: for a very long time.

yesterday

to be born yesterday: to be easily deceived.

yarn

to spin a yarn: to tell a story, usually untrue.